Getaway GUIDE TO
wildlife
photography

Nigel Dennis

SUNBIRD
PUBLISHING

First published 2002
2 4 6 8 10 9 7 5 3

Sunbird Publishing (Pty) Ltd
34 Sunset Avenue, Llandudno, Cape Town, South Africa
Registration number: 4850177827

Publisher Dick Wilkins
Editor Brenda Brickman
Designer Mandy McKay
Production Manager Andrew de Kock

Reproduction by Unifoto (Pty) Ltd, Cape Town
Printed and bound by Tien Wah Press (Pte) Ltd, Singapore

ISBN 0 624 04064 X

PREVIOUS PAGE *Flash and natural light were combined to create this atmospheric image of a caracal at sunset.*
ABOVE *An assassin bug photographed in the author's back garden – proof that you don't*
necessarily need to visit exotic reserves to find interesting photo subjects.
OPPOSITE *Sunset over northern Kruger. A polarising filter was used to enhance and saturate the sky colour.*

CONTENTS

INTRODUCTION

The most highly prized of big game photo subjects, this leopard had carried her impala prey into a marula tree. A 600mm f4 lens was used to keep a good working distance and avoid disturbing the animal.

Why is wildlife photography such a popular pastime? The answers are many. Wildlife photography can be a rewarding means of artistic expression. And there is the satisfying challenge of learning the specialised skills that are required of a successful wildlife photographer.

If we are honest, the thrill of the 'hunt' also plays a significant role in the popularity of wildlife photography. The best thing about hunting with a camera is that the instinct can be fulfilled without the hunter having to kill. Lastly – and I believe this is possibly the most rewarding aspect – wildlife photography is a wonderful means of making contact with the natural world. To capture even a little of nature's beauty on film is immensely gratifying.

So, what do you need to do to take good quality wildlife photographs? You don't necessarily have to have the most expensive camera on the market, although an excellent lens is essential.

Luck can play a part, of course, and Gary Player put 'luck' into perspective very nicely: 'The more I practise, the luckier I get.' Undoubtedly this applies as much to wildlife photography as it does to golf.

Practice is essential if you are to fine-tune the skills required to make the most of every opportunity. For this reason the greater part of this book concentrates on photographic techniques. My aim is to help you to take control of the photographic medium, rather than encouraging you to simply be relieved when some of your pictures turn out satisfactorily.

I have kept the technical jargon intentionally short. Wildlife photography should be fun, and you don't need an enormous amount of technical knowledge to do it well.

The trick though, is to know how to apply camera basics, such as shutter speed, aperture, exposure and choice of lens, and how to make these work for you.

In this book I also look at the use of filters to enhance natural colour, and offer some useful flash and reflector techniques to improve the appearance of an image when natural lighting is less than ideal.

The bottom line is this: you don't *take* worthwhile wildlife pictures, you *make* them!

South Africa, which harbours so many fantastic game and nature reserves, offers the most brilliant opportunities for wildlife photography. I have offered information on what I think are some of the best reserves in the country. Within each reserve there are specific times of the year when you are likely to achieve the best photographic results, and these I have also mentioned.

In South Africa's abundant reserves it is relatively easy to spot game at a distance. However, getting within a

'The more I practise, the luckier I get,' certainly applies to wildlife photography. In 16 years I have had just one opportunity to get this close to the wild and wary saddle-billed stork.

suitable range to take a viable picture of an animal is a different story, so I've included 10 tips to help you find and get close enough to exciting photo subjects to take a great photograph. I have also suggested where you should go if there is a particular species of animal that you would like to capture on film.

Lastly, a word on the picture captions. A lot of photographers are curious about the technical information related to a photograph – what camera, lens, film, shutter speed and aperture are used, and so on. I have not included the camera models in the captions, as I don't believe this is particularly important. I have, however, offered the lens focal length, as differing perspectives and depths of field greatly influence the appearance of an image.

Film type is pretty standard throughout. Ninety-five percent of the time I've used Fujichrome Velvia 50ASA, and for the rest Provia 100ASA. I don't generally record shutter speed and aperture (an impractical task as I shoot up to 800 rolls of film a year!), so I have only included these where I could clearly recall the details, and the information seemed pertinent.

Wishing you good luck, and great wildlife photographs!

My set-up for the leopard photo opposite. Note the steady camera support for the big lens, and on the left a powerful flash that helped to fill shadows in the harsh light.

Nigel Dennis

PHOTOGRAPHIC EQUIPMENT

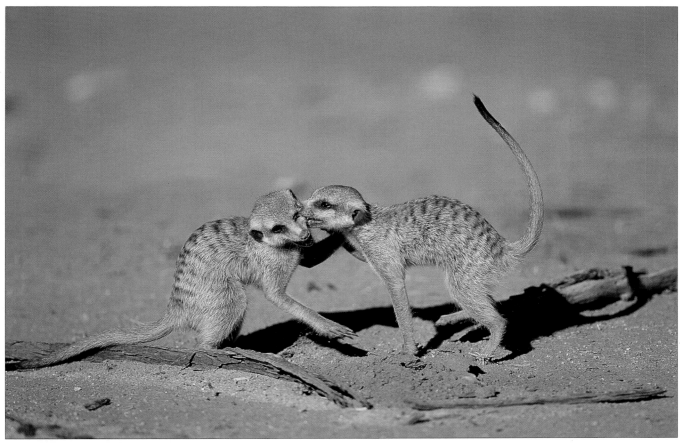

This image of young meerkats at play was taken with an inexpensive and fairly battered old camera. What made the shot was an excellent lens – a Canon 70–200mm f2.8L zoom – which incorporated super-fast auto-focus.

CAMERAS

Although a modern 35mm camera is loaded with electronic options, the essential function of a camera body remains the same today as it was 50 years ago: it is, primarily, a light tight box designed to hold film. For this reason I would urge photo enthusiasts not to spend a fortune on a camera, but rather to buy the very best lenses. If you need to skimp a bit, do so on the camera. After all, it is really the lens that takes and makes the picture.

Even an inexpensive basic camera, when coupled to an excellent lens, will produce some fine images. Put a mediocre lens on the most advanced 'top of the range' camera body and the best you can ever expect are mediocre pictures.

The majority of features that you need to produce excellent photographs are present in most of the low-budget, 'entry-level' cameras produced by the better-known manufacturers.

The basic camera requirements are, firstly, an exposure system that gives you some control over the camera, or at least more control than you would have with a fully automated mode system. An aperture priority programme, where you manually select the aperture and the on-board electronics automatically set the appropriate shutter speed, is ideal.

A complete manual override option, allowing both shutter speed and aperture to be controlled by the photographer, is also handy.

Another important feature is the facility to attach a cable release. This is vital to taking sharp pictures with long telephoto lenses, and when using slow exposures with any lens.

Useful extras would include dial-in exposure compensation for both the camera and the flash, and a stop-down preview button – although this last one is by no means essential.

Almost all current camera models incorporate auto-focus. The more basic cameras have between one and three focus-sensing areas within the viewfinder. Once again, this is perfectly adequate. Some of my 'top end' cameras have multiple focusing points – dozens in fact. But I find I seldom use any other than the central points and the ones just off-centre to the left and right. These are exactly the same focusing points that are present in the cheaper models!

When comparing cameras, it is a good idea to check on the ease with which it is possible to switch the selected auto-focus points. In some models this is a fiddling process – not the kind of thing you would want to have to bother with when a cheetah is about to pounce on an impala right in front of you!

When you buy a new camera body, be sure to read the instruction manual. This may sound like an obvious and unnecessary piece of advice (and I agree that a camera manual is hardly riveting reading), but it is essential that you know how everything works before you set out on a field trip. It is a good idea to spend some time playing around with the camera at home to ensure that you understand each of the controls. Also, make sure that you know how to use all of the functions that may need to be altered on a photo shoot. These include setting the ASA speed, selecting an exposure mode, and tweaking the settings for flash and camera exposure compensations.

At some stage you will most likely want to upgrade your basic camera body to a more sophisticated and advanced model (many photo enthusiasts end up becoming avid collectors of photo gear!).

Be sure to hang onto your basic camera though – it will always be useful as a backup on photo safaris. Having more than one camera body also reduces time wastage when changing lenses, and will certainly result in fewer missed opportunities.

TELEPHOTO LENSES

Do you need to have a super-powerful telephoto lens to take good pictures of African wildlife? Not necessarily, but it certainly helps, especially in the southern African national parks, where off-road driving is not allowed.

I would guess that I have at least 25 000 images of African animals and birds in my photo library. Of these, probably about half were taken with lenses of 600mm or more. For most of the remainder I used 300mm to 500mm lenses, with only a small proportion of images shot with lenses of 200mm or below. Of course, a long

A 100–300mm zoom is light and versatile. This zoom range works well for general game photography, as well as with the more confiding birds, such as the pied kingfisher shown here.

Budget for the longest good telephoto that you can afford. This Ethiopian snipe was photographed with a good 500mm f4.5 lens coupled to a basic – and now obsolete – model of camera.

Although expensive, 'fast glass', helps in low-light conditions. A super-fast 300mm f2.8 was used at its widest aperture for this white rhino portrait – taken in the last drop of the day's light.

lens is a real boon in bird photography, because small, skittish subjects are often difficult to approach.

If you are at all serious about wildlife photography, a primary objective should be to acquire a telephoto of at least 300mm. A 400mm or 500mm lens would be even better, and, if your budget can run to it, a 600mm lens would be very useful indeed.

The ultimate lens for wildlife photography is probably a 600mm f4. At 600mm you get an impressive 12× magnification. The 'fast' f4 aperture gathers plenty of light to shoot action with 100ASA or even 50ASA fine-grained films. However, this is a huge piece of equipment,

weighing up to six kilograms, and unfortunately carries an equally hefty price tag – one which, at local prices, is equivalent to that of a perfectly acceptable new car! Apart from the very wealthy, or a person intending to make a living from photography, I think few could justify this kind of expenditure.

Fortunately there have been some remarkable advances in optical technology in recent years. This means that it is now possible to get quality super-telephoto magnification at a fraction of the cost of a hefty 600mm f4.

A teleconverter – also known as a tele-extender – is an additional optical unit that is placed between the lens and camera to increase magnification. Today most of the main camera manufacturers produce teleconverters (matched to their telelenses) of such superb quality that it is difficult to tell that a teleconverter has been used.

If you start with a 300mm f2.8 lens and add a 2× converter, the combination effectively becomes a 600mm f5.6 lens. At f5.6 the lens still has enough light-gathering power to take action shots.

The 300mm f2.8 lens can also be matched with a 1.4× converter, producing a very serviceable 420mm f4. In fact, a 300mm f2.8 with the two converters makes an excellent and versatile wildlife photography outfit.

My wife and I work together and sometimes photograph the same subjects using a 600mm f4 and a 300mm f2.8 with 2× converter respectively (I must admit I generally commandeer the 600mm f4!). When we have our films processed, there is often some dispute over who took which pictures, as the results are so similar in sharpness and colour saturation. A 300mm f2.8 and converter costs less than half the 600mm f4, yet the results are virtually indistinguishable.

Moving along in the affordability stakes, a slower 300mm can also be combined with a teleconverter. If you add a 1.4× converter to a 300mm f4 lens, it becomes a 420mm f5.6. An added advantage is that this is a lightweight, portable outfit that can be easily carried all day – an excellent choice for anyone wishing to combine some serious hiking with equally serious photography! The cost should be less than one-eighth of the price of a 600mm f4 lens.

The older teleconverters were not much good, but if you buy new, or at least latest-technology equipment made by a prime camera manufacturer, this outfit will give outstanding results.

While it is possible to put a 2× converter on a 300mm f4, the two-stop light-loss from the converter makes this

Teleconverters matched with modern telephoto lenses are a good combination. This tight shot of a shy kori bustard required a 600mm f4 coupled with a 1.4× teleconverter – effectively making the lens a super-powerful 840mm f5.6.

combination a 600mm f8 – which is a bit too slow for anything other than static animal or bird portraits.

In recent years many keen photographers have switched to auto-focus – so there are a lot of perfectly good manual-focus lenses on the secondhand market. These could be a worthwhile option for those on a tight budget. However, always insist on testing a secondhand lens thoroughly before purchase; at a glance a lens might look okay, but a bad knock may have upset the alignment of internal optics.

For super-magnification at a real budget price, you could go for a secondhand Novaflex lens. Once the mainstay of many wildlife photographers, the Novaflex (which incidentally is a long-focus lens rather than a true telephoto, as it utilises only one group of optics) has been somewhat overtaken by the new generation optics. There are many serviceable secondhand Novaflexes on the market, which can produce very acceptable results.

If you shop around a bit, some wonderful bargains can be found. A friend, warning me that he was on a strictly limited budget, recently asked me to keep a lookout for a cheap telelens. After a phone call to my local camera store I located a battered, but functioning 400mm f5.6

Novaflex – for an unbelievable R200! The lens coating sported a bit of fungus, which we carefully cleaned, but otherwise it worked just fine. It's not every day that you can get started in wildlife photography for the equivalent cost of four rolls of film!

A pygmy goose photographed with a 300mm f2.8 lens and 2× teleconverter, a cost-effective combination that turned the lens into a 600mm f5.6, resulting in quality super-magnification.

Tiny reptiles, such as this web-footed gecko, require a lens capable of focusing at very close range. A specialised macro lens is ideal, although very acceptable results are also possible with a standard 50mm lens and extension tube.

ZOOMS, WIDE-ANGLE LENSES AND MACRO LENSES

The fixed-focal length long telephoto tends to be the 'standard' lens of the wildlife photographer. However, it is important and useful to add a variety of shorter lenses to your photo kit. This will enable you to successfully portray a wide range of subject matter in a variety of situations. Ideally you should aim at putting together a range of lenses to cover everything from close-up work, showing landscapes and animals 'in environment', right through to the super-telephotos required for tight shots of animals and birds.

The optical performance of current telephoto zoom lenses is outstanding. I include several zooms in my standard photo kit and find that they produce images of much the same sharpness and colour saturation as my fixed-focal length lenses. The most popular zoom is the 70–200mm. Many photographers, after buying their first camera body (usually supplied with a standard 50mm lens), will opt for this focal length. The 70–200mm does have a fair variety of applications for wildlife photos although the moderate 200mm magnification is a little limiting. If your main interest is wildlife, then a 100–300mm zoom would be more useful.

Some manufacturers now offer the 100–400mm range of focal lengths as well. Generally, such zooms have a maximum aperture of f5.6 or f6.7 – a bit on the slow side, but this is a fair trade-off as these lenses have the advantage of being light and portable.

A few manufacturers produce super-telephoto zooms, usually with focal lengths in the 200–600mm range.

A 50mm macro is fine for plant close-ups, but 100mm or 200mm macros are better for more skittish subjects. I used a 100mm f4 macro for this shot of a rare Madagascar tomato frog.

A 70–200mm zoom is handy for showing animals in their environment. Experiment with the zoom function to achieve a good balance. This giraffe image was taken mid-morning, so I added a polarising filter to saturate the blue sky and enhance the clouds.

These are costly optics, but the ability to zoom straight from medium to super-telephoto magnification makes for quick, easy framing – particularly useful when the action is fast and furious. On the downside, such zooms have rather slow maximum apertures – f5.6 or f6.7. Also, if you plan to photograph on hiking trails, a super-telephoto zoom would be awfully bulky and heavy to cart around. My preference would be to opt for the faster fixed telelenses (matched with teleconverters when extra power is required) mentioned earlier, and add a 100–300mm zoom to cover the shorter focal lengths.

When photographing 'on foot' I seldom carry anything heavier than a 100–300mm zoom.

Wide-angle lenses are wonderful for taking photos of creatures in their environment, as well as for scenic photography. For many years I owned only one lens in this category – a moderately wide 24mm. This inexpensive lens served me very well and was only replaced a few years ago with a 20–35mm zoom. Last year I added a 17–35mm to the collection – a bit pricey but the flexibility in coverage from super-wide to moderately wide is very handy.

Close-ups of bugs and flowers require some specialist equipment. The cheapest way to take close-ups is to place an extension tube between your camera and lens.

This smallish camera bag accommodates almost everything I need on a photo trip, from a 17–35mm super-wide zoom to a 600mm telephoto (a 300mm f2.8 coupled with a 2× teleconverter).

A powerful flash system is essential for nocturnal animal portraits. This aardvark was captured with a Metz 60CT4 flash (guide number 60) and a flash beam intensifier that acts like a big magnifying glass to concentrate illumination from the flash.

Extension tubes have no optics, so an inexpensive one purchased from an independent manufacturer will probably work just fine. Make sure, however, that it is matched to your camera system so that fully automatic functions are maintained.

I was able to approach these meerkats closely enough for some shots with a wide-angle lens. The small flash on top of the camera was sufficient to add a little fill at such short range.

The specially designed macro lenses are the 'Rolls Royce' of lenses when doing close-up work. Macro lenses focus very close without the aid of an extension tube. Also, optics are set up to produce excellent sharpness at very short distances. They are available in 50mm, 100mm and 200mm. The 100mm and 200mm lenses have a greater working range, especially for photographing skittish insects such as butterflies.

The last word on lenses is that if you are at all serious about wildlife photography, always buy the best lenses you can afford. Otherwise you are sure to want to upgrade in the future. I have done a lot of buying and selling of lenses in the past and, goodness knows, it can become an expensive business!

FLASH UNITS

Flash is an invaluable accessory for the wildlife and nature photographer. Apart from facilitating night photography, flash can improve the look of images taken in harsh or poor light, and also open up the fascinating field of macros and close-ups.

I used a 600mm f4 lens to get a tight framing on these wild dogs, and added fill to a potentially badly light- and shade-dappled shot with a powerful Metz 60CT4 flash and beam intensifier.

When purchasing a flash system it is important to obtain one that has sufficient reach and power to be used outdoors. Also, if your budget can possibly run to it, a TTL system – that is, a flash that will make automatic exposures 'through the lens' by utilising the camera's metering system – will make the job a whole lot easier.

Flash units are calibrated with a manufacturer's 'guide number', which gives an indication of the unit's power and thus the distance it can illuminate. Unfortunately the claims for flash reach are based on indoor use, where scattered light will bounce off the ceiling and walls. Outside there is little to reflect light, thereby reducing the distance that the flash is capable of illuminating. Generally, you can almost halve the manufacturer's claims for effective flash distance when photographing outside. For this reason, a small flash gun that would work just fine for family snaps at home, will be of very little use when photographing animals at night or for the daylight-fill flash techniques described in later chapters.

At a pinch, you can take night shots of animals by using a small flash system along with a very fast film (800ASA or above), but the resulting images will be grainy and have poor colour. Try to aim for a flash system with a guide number of at least 45. I have used Metz flashes for the past 20 years or so, and my current flash is the 60CT4, and the guide number is the same as the model, in other words, 60.

While on the subject of flash systems, it is well worth purchasing a couple of very useful accessories. Firstly, an off-camera lead will allow the flash to be positioned a short distance away from the camera. A flash unit positioned away from your camera will entirely eliminate the 'red-eye' effect so often seen on family snapshots taken with a 'point and shoot'. If your flash operates with automatic TTL metering, it is important to purchase a dedicated lead that allows these functions to operate off-camera as well.

A second very useful accessory is a teleflash beam intensifier. Teleflash attachments increase range by utilising a Freschnel lens to concentrate and narrow the flash beam – rather like putting a big magnifying glass in front of the flash.

For this sunset silhouette of a Kalahari gemsbok I used a 300mm f2.8 lens and 1.4× teleconverter, as well as a solid camera support and cable release to prevent blurring at such a low shutter speed.

A beanbag makes an excellent ground-level support – much easier than trying to adjust a tripod to such a low angle. 'Worm's-eye view' photography can produce striking, impressive images.

The models I have tried are marketed in the States as the Project-a-Flash, made by George Lepp, and the Visual Echoes Flash Extender from Kirk Enterprises. These can be difficult to obtain in South Africa, so it helps if you have a friend over there. Alternatively, you can order it through the Internet. Luckily flash extenders are not expensive and are light to post.

For Metz users, a teleflash attachment that fits the Metz 60 range is available. I have used this for many years. While the light gain is not as great as the Lepp and Kirk products, the beam is less narrow and so does not have to be as accurately directed – very helpful when tracking a moving subject.

CAMERA SUPPORTS AND TRIPODS

Foremost among photo accessories are camera supports for use in a vehicle, and when photographing on foot or from a hide. Let's take a look at car camera supports first. The most basic type of support when photographing from a car is a beanbag. Beanbags offer a number of advantages. They are cheap (they are easily made at home) and will fit over the open window of any type of vehicle – useful if you are hiring a vehicle or if you are on an escorted game drive and you don't know beforehand how much room will be available to you. You don't necessarily have to fill the bag with beans; when travelling you can carry an empty cloth bag and fill it with gravel when you reach your photographic destination. It is handy to have different-sized bags: a small one for lenses of up to 200mm, and a huge beanbag for supporting lenses of 500mm and more.

A bean bag is very stable for taking static shots but can be awkward when trying to pan smoothly to follow a fast-moving subject. For this reason I use a fluid-action video head for all my telephoto work from a vehicle. The problem arises in finding a really sturdy vehicle support for the video head.

Commercially made car camera support brackets are available, and are okay for lenses up to 400mm or, at a push, 500mm. I stopped using a camera bracket some years ago when I had a 600mm lens topple over and tumble – lens first – into the Kalahari sand! Fortunately, no damage was done. Since then, however, I have had a welded bracket constructed and bolted firmly and permanently inside my car door. It made a bit of a mess of the interior of a new four-by-four, but at least I have had no more unhappy accidents with expensive lenses falling out of the window! I can understand that not

In Kaokoland, I discovered this fairly tame francolin. However the bird would only allow me to get within 600mm range. A heavy tripod and cable release were essential to avoid camera shake that would have otherwise blurred the image when using such a long lens.

everyone would welcome the idea of such a permanent fixture on the family vehicle, in which case a proprietary car camera bracket would be the next best thing.

Tripods are essential when using long lenses from a hide or when on foot. A tripod is also important when taking slow exposures with any kind of lens. A medium-weight tripod will usually suffice for lenses up to 600mm. Don't go in for tripod overkill, or you will end up with something that is so heavy that you will not want to bother to carry it around.

I have used a Benbo tripod for the last two decades. The Benbo utilises a kind of universal joint that allows the legs to be set up easily on uneven ground.

The lower legs are also waterproof, so there is no problem using the tripod in mud or shallow water.

I also carry a cheap, lightweight tripod for landscape and nature shots when I expect to be hiking some

distance. If used with a bit of care, the lightweight version is fine for wide-angles or even short telephoto lenses.

It is well worth investing in two types of heads to go on the tripod. For landscape and close-up work most photographers opt for a ball head or a three-way pan-tilt head. I much prefer the latter as it makes the task of getting the camera level much easier. I also find changing from a horizontal to vertical framing on the camera less fiddling than with a ball head.

When you expect to be following fast action by panning with telelenses, then a fluid-action head is a big advantage. Even the best ball heads tend to be too jerky for the accurate smooth panning that is vital when tracking a subject with auto-focus. The fluid-action head I favour is the Manfrotto Model 136. This is an inexpensive head designed for video work, although it also works exceptionally well for telephoto stills photography.

A 100ASA slide film offers a good compromise – fine grain, good colour and a workable speed. It is worth experimenting with different brands under various lighting conditions. I used Fuji Astia 100ASA for this close-up, and it handled the harsh afternoon light rather well.

FILM CHOICES –
PRINTS, SLIDES OR DIGITAL?

I am often asked, 'What is the best film to take on an African photo safari?'

The short answer is that it depends mainly on what you might want to use your photos for in the future and, to a certain extent, on the type of gear you possess.

Film choices today also include the new medium of digital photography. Digital has some significant pros and cons that we will examine later, but first, let's take a look at the options available in conventional film.

The first decision is to opt for print (negative) or slide (transparency) film.

If your primary interest is to make economical, quality print enlargements from your work, then print film is the way to go. The great advantage of print film is that it is very forgiving in terms of exposure. Even if your exposures are a little off the mark, it is still possible to salvage an acceptable print.

The main drawback is that it is not possible to assess the quality of an image by looking at a processed roll of negatives, making it necessary to either have a contact sheet printed, or to have postcard-sized prints made of the entire roll. This adds substantially to cost.

Slide film has the advantage of producing beautifully saturated colours and excellent detail. It should be your first choice if you intend to submit your work for publication, or if you wish to enter the big photo competitions. Of course, it will also allow you to present your work as a slide show.

The cost of processing a roll of slide film is quite reasonable – not a small consideration if you plan to shoot many rolls on a photo trip. It is also possible to have excellent prints made from slide film, either by a conventional photographic process such as Cibachrome, or by having the slide scanned and digitally printed. However, good prints from slides tend to be expensive, so this is a definite disadvantage if you intend to have a lot of prints made.

The main disadvantage of slide film is that it requires very meticulous and precise exposure. Images that are too light or too dark are essentially 'throw outs', as nothing can be done to correct exposure errors after the film has been processed.

The next question is whether you should go for a fast film or a slow film.

Fast films allow high shutter speeds, making it possible to hand-hold a telephoto lens and, at the same time, utilise the freezing action. The trade-off is that these films – particularly 400ASA and above – have noticeable grain along with high contrast and less saturated colours.

Slow film needs more care in avoiding camera shake, but tends to have little grain and natural, attractive colour. Very slow films – such as the 'benchmark' Fujichrome Velvia 50ASA – produce images of exceptional quality, and for this reason are much favoured by professional wildlife photographers. Such slow films are, however, very limiting unless you possess fast lenses with maximum apertures of f2.8 or, at most, f4. A slower lens, such as a f5.6 or f6.7, will not gather enough light to allow you to freeze action when used with 50ASA film. For most wildlife photography 100ASA is a good compromise, and one that is workable with f5.6 lenses.

The latest 100ASA films have fine grain and excellent colour. In fact, the results are very close to the 'benchmark' 50ASA films.

My advice would be to stick with 100ASA for most wildlife work, but carry a few rolls of fast 400ASA for very low-light situations and to obtain extra reach when shooting flash at night.

Digital technology has improved vastly in recent years. Advantages of shooting digital include zero film costs, as well as being able to view the picture straight after it has been taken, and so keeping only those images that you are satisfied with.

There is also a great deal that can be done to tweak or improve a digital images. Working in the 'digital darkroom' and utilising programmes such as PhotoShop can be a lot of fun, with plenty of scope for creativity. While the imaging technology will never turn a poor picture into a great one, it does allow the photographer to make a good image look even better. Corrections to colour and contrast can easily be made, and it is also possible, to a certain extent, to sharpen pictures that are a little 'soft'.

At the moment, digital 35mm cameras have one big drawback – cost. A good digital camera will set you back two to three times the cost of a conventional camera. You will also need a fast computer with plenty of RAM, some fairly expensive software, and a high-quality colour printer if you want to enhance and print your images at home.

Velvia 50ASA is a slow film and requires a fast lens as well as a steady support. Here I used my 600mm 'wide open' at f4 to give just enough speed to get the shot in low light.

I was able to get a shutter speed of 1/1500 sec at f4 – just fast enough to freeze the wing beats of this pale chanting goshawk – on a Provia 100ASA film.

Close-ups generally require good depth of field. The trade-off is that small apertures mean slow shutter speeds, so I had to wait until this anthid beetle was absolutely still before taking the image.

This Egyptian goose was in take-off mode so I took the shot with my 600mm lens wide open at f4 to get the highest possible shutter speed. Note the very limited depth of field.

SHUTTER SPEED AND APERTURE – UNDERSTANDING THE BASICS

Wildlife photography is an extremely rewarding pastime, bringing with it a fantastic sense of achievement.

However, while I think that it is unnecessary for photographers to become bogged down with technical information, there is one fundamental concept that I believe all photographers need to understand. It concerns the relationship between shutter speed and aperture. Mastering this basic law of optics will enable you to take control of your photographic results and achieve the kind of pictures you want to make – rather than just being pleasantly surprised when your shots turn out 'okay'.

Please take the trouble to read through this chapter – I promise I will make it as simple and non-technical as I possibly can!

Under any given circumstances there will be a certain amount of light that will be required to pass through the lens and fall onto the film in order to expose it satisfactorily. Your camera controls or regulates this exposure in two ways.

Firstly, by the length of time that the shutter stays open. This can be determined by the shutter speeds you see on your camera controls – 1/500, 1/250, 1/125 sec, and so on. And secondly, by opening up or closing down the iris diaphragm in the lens, which is known as lens aperture. This is calibrated in numbered 'f-stops', for example, f2.8, f4, f5.6, f8, f11, f16, and so forth.

I am sure you will have noticed that the shutter speeds either double or halve as you click through on the camera controls. And, as you change the aperture on the lens, the amount of light that can pass through the lens will *also* double or halve accordingly for each f-stop.

The higher the f-stop number, the smaller the opening in the iris diaphragm. So, for example, f5.6 will halve the amount of light that would have passed through at f4. Opening up the aperture to the next widest f-stop (f2.8) will double the amount of light that falls on the film.

To practise, focus your camera on a medium-sized animal, such as an impala. Press the shutter button down halfway to activate the metering. For argument's sake, let's say you get an exposure reading of 1/500 sec at an aperture of f8. (The most convenient way to conduct this test is with the camera set on aperture priority mode – so you select the aperture and the camera gives the corresponding shutter speed.)

By changing the f-stop down to f11 the camera will automatically double the duration that the shutter stays open to 1/250 sec. Similarly, f16 will give you 1/125 sec and f22 will read 1/60 sec.

You could go the other way and open up the lens to f5.6. The camera will then halve the speed to 1/1000 sec.

Open up another stop to f4, and you will get a shutter speed of 1/2000 sec.

The important thing to remember is that all of these readings will allow the same amount of light to fall on the film – so you will get *exactly the same exposure.*

Although extreme settings of f4 at 1/2000 sec and f22 at 1/60 give similar exposures, the resulting images will look very different. As a lens is stopped down by the application of a higher f-stop number, the 'depth of field' increases. (The depth of field is the zone of acceptable sharpness in front of and behind the area that has been precisely focused.)

Assuming you are using an f-stop of f4 and have focused on the head of the impala, the hindquarters of the animal (if facing away from you) would probably be out of focus. Certainly the bush behind the animal and the grass in front of it will both be out of focus.

Without altering focus, take exactly the same picture at f22, and you will see that the entire impala will be in

focus, as will much of the background and foreground. The only problem is that at f22 (which you will remember required a slow 1/60 sec exposure), had the impala decided to move as you took the picture, it would appear blurred in the image. The lens may have been correctly focused but the slow shutter speed would not have frozen the animal's movement.

You will need to opt for a fast shutter speed to freeze action, but with a very limited zone of sharp focus. Otherwise, go for a small aperture to give lots of depth of field, but without a sufficiently high shutter speed to freeze the subject if it happens to be moving.

Unfortunately, other than using a very fast film that will result in grainy images, there is no way around this problem. The good news is that what may at first appear to be a limitation of the photographic medium can, in fact, be turned around and used as a creative tool. We will look at some techniques that can be used to do this in the following pages.

In order to capture foreground-to-horizon sharpness in this Kalahari scene, I used a 20mm lens stopped all the way down to f22. The corresponding shutter speed of 1/15sec meant that I had to wait for a lull in the wind in order to get a sharp image of the devil's thorn flower in the foreground.

For this impala and oxpecker shot I used my 600mm lens stopped down to f5.6, giving sufficient depth of field to keep both their heads sharp, leaving the background unobtrusive.

This crisp image of a baboon feeding on mopane leaves was achieved with a 600mm lens used wide open at f4. The blurred background makes the subject stand out clearly.

USE THE TELEPHOTO ADVANTAGE TO GIVE YOUR IMAGES THE 'PRO' LOOK

As we have now seen, the depth of field (apparent sharpness) increases when a lens is stopped down to a smaller aperture. This zone of apparent sharpness also differs with the *focal length of a lens*. Wide-angle lenses of less than 35mm have a far greater depth of apparent sharpness than that of, for example, a 300mm telephoto. Very long telephoto lenses – 600mm and above – have an extremely limited depth of sharpness. Even when stopped down to the smallest available aperture the depth of field is minute. Does this mean that long telelenses make for bad wildlife photography? Not at all. The trick is to make that limited depth of field work for you, so that your images have a professional look about them.

One of the problems encountered when taking photographs of African wildlife (or for that matter, wildlife photography just about anywhere) is the amount of 'clutter' found on the landscape. This is most apparent in the thick bush and dense grass cover typical of the Kruger National Park and the Zululand reserves.

It is often difficult to make a lion appear to stand out from the tawny grass cover of winter, or a leopard visible when photographed in dense bush. The telephoto's shallow depth of field then becomes the photographer's greatest ally.

When photographing in dense cover I often opt for my longest lens, and shoot 'wide open' at the largest aperture. The clutter in front of and behind the subject is then reduced to an out-of-focus 'mist' – much like a colour wash in a watercolour painting. With all the clutter out of the way, the subject then appears to jump right out of the frame.

This is such a useful technique that I sometimes take it to extremes and use my 600mm f4 – which happens to be my longest lens – coupled with a 1.4× converter. Effectively this outfit becomes an 840mm f5.6 with exceptionally shallow depth of field – capable of producing crisp, clean images in even the scrappiest bush.

The telephoto's shallow depth of field does, however, need to be used with some care. In particular, your focus on the subject has to be absolutely spot-on. The precision of auto-focus helps of course, but even with the latest gear, simply pointing the lens and hoping for the best is not good enough.

When the subject is large in the frame – such as with a head-and-shoulders portrait – focusing just anywhere on

I only had a second or two to get my lens onto this hovering black-shouldered kite. I always leave my camera setting on the widest aperture and continuous auto-focus. This allowed me to grab the shot without wasting time in fiddling with the controls.

the subject will not suffice. The main thing is to ensure that the eye of the animal is in perfect focus. If, for example, the tip of the animal's nose appears a little soft but the eye is pin sharp, the picture will probably work just fine. The other way around and the shot would most likely best be consigned to the waste bin.

In fact, as a general rule you should focus on the eye when taking tightly framed pictures, and you will not go far wrong.

An important note for auto-focus users. When taking static portraits – such as a head shot of a giraffe standing and staring at the camera – it is best to use the focus lock mode (also known as 'one shot' mode). This will allow you to focus accurately on the animal's eye, and to hold the same focus as you reframe the image to make an attractive and balanced composition. However, if the giraffe begins to browse on a nearby acacia, you will probably not have time to focus lock and reframe before the animal has moved a little and is out of precise focus.

Moving subjects are best tracked with continuous auto-focus ('servo' mode), although composition would then be restricted by the available auto-focus points on your camera.

GETTING REALLY SHARP

Achieving pin-sharp photographs is not difficult. All that is needed is a little care, and two fairly basic pieces of photo gear, which we will discuss a little further on.

I photographed this Kalahari cheetah with my 600mm lens supported by a huge beanbag. A cable release eliminated the chance of blurring the image with camera shake.

A bird park picture of a vulturine guineafowl taken with a hand-held 300mm f4 image-stabilising lens. The shutter speed was 1/60 sec and the f11 aperture gave lots of depth of field.

Image-stabilising lenses offer mobility – you don't have to carry around a heavy tripod. This technology produces sharp images at lower shutter speed than is possible with a conventional lens.

Firstly though, let's take a look at the least efficient way to take a photograph – that is, to hand-hold a camera. No matter how steady you think your grip might be, there will inevitably be a certain amount of movement that will soften the image. Some situations, however, such as a 'grab shot' of fast animal action or behaviour, demand hand-holding because there is simply not enough time to set up a tripod. Better to take a stab at hand-holding the camera than miss the shot entirely.

At such times, it would be wise to use this rough practice as a guideline to hand-holding: if you ensure that the shutter speed of the camera is the *same or greater* than the lens focal length, then you should have a fair success rate.

A 500mm lens, for example, could be hand-held with reasonable success at a shutter speed of 1/500 sec. A 24mm wide angle could be hand-held at 1/30 sec (the closest available speed to 24). At best, I feel that hand-holding a camera is a bit 'iffy'. And while most shots will be fairly sharp using this lens and shutter speed ratio, often there will not be sufficient light to achieve the required speed at the preferred aperture. Also, using a camera support will make for a considerably better composition – especially when using telephotos, where the slightest movement of the lens will greatly alter the framing of the image.

If you want to be certain of image sharpness you need just two pieces of equipment – a tripod (or similar support) and a cable release – it's as simple as that. Using a tripod on its own is already a great improvement over hand-holding, but manually pressing the shutter button can easily introduce a little unsteadiness into the system. By adding the cable release you will be able to achieve true 'hands-off' photography – the sure way to make pin-sharp pictures.

With wide-angle to short telephoto lenses you can get good results with a fairly lightweight and cheap tripod. Longer lenses require something sturdier, and huge telephoto lenses of 600mm and above will need a pretty hefty tripod to ensure stability. While it is not much fun to carry this kit around – such a set-up could easily weigh 20 kilograms, if you include the lens – there is little option if it's a sharp image you're after.

Beanbags and monopods are more portable alternatives. I use beanbags often. They are handy when photographing from a vehicle and excellent when you need to shoot at ground level (tricky and awkward with many tripods).

A young lion photographed with the sun on the horizon. I used a 600mm f4 lens at its widest aperture. The shutter speed, with Velvia 50ASA film, was only 1/15 sec, and required a good camera support and a cable release to prevent camera shake.

A beanbag of a size that is lens-appropriate can be as stable as a good tripod – and is, of course, far cheaper. There is, however, one major disadvantage to using a beanbag: I find that it is extremely difficult to pan smoothly from it. For this reason I tend to use beanbags mainly for static subjects.

Monopods are popular with many photographers. I agree that they are less of a nuisance to cart around than a tripod, but I don't seem to get on well with them. You might get away with a shutter speed of say 1/125 sec with a 500mm lens on a monopod – if you are *very* careful. To be on the safe side 1/250 or 1/500 sec would result in a better percentage of sharp shots.

So, to my mind, the advantages of a monopod over hand-holding are minimal. I would rather try to do the job properly, and carry a tripod.

In recent years, image-stabilising (IS) lenses have become available. The on-board electronics optically detect movement ('shake') of the lens, rather than sensing physical movement or vibration, and compensate by adjusting internal lens elements.

I have used a 300mm f4 IS lens quite extensively. It is a lightweight piece of equipment and has proved useful when it is not practical to use or carry a tripod (or on occasions when I am just feeling plain lazy!).

My feeling is that the image-stabilising function offers about a two-stop advantage over hand-holding. In other words, with the IS engaged, I find I can achieve an acceptable percentage of sharp pictures at 1/60 sec, whereas a 300mm telephoto would normally need a shutter speed of at least 1/250 sec when hand-held.

However, in my experience, IS lenses are not infallible, so as things stand at the moment, lugging around a tripod – cumbersome as it may be – and using a cable release is still the surest way to achieve really sharp images.

Blurred pan images give a convincing impression of speed. I used a shutter speed of 1/15 sec on this young spotted hyena running flat out. Such images work best when the legs and body blur, but the head of the animal appears sharp.

SHOOTING ACTION: FREEZE OR BLUR?

Action and behavioural images present a great challenge to the photographer. Before we look at techniques and accessories, it is important to decide up front what it is that we are trying to achieve in action images.

There are two ways in which one could approach action photography. One is to attempt to freeze a moment in time by using a high shutter speed. The second is to

The wing beats of large birds, such as these lappet-faced vultures, are fairly slow. I was able to capture this sharp action image at 1/750 sec. Smaller birds would require a far higher shutter speed.

forget about freezing the image and go for an impression of speed or movement – known as a 'blurred pan'.

The shutter speed required to freeze action depends on the speed and size of the subject and, to an extent, the direction in which it is travelling.

Large birds, such as eagles and vultures, and medium-to large-sized mammals do not require exceptionally high shutter speeds. If the subject is running or flying across the frame, a shutter speed of 1/500 to 1/1000 sec will work. Should the subject be moving directly towards the camera, a slower speed will still result in a frozen image, and you could probably get away with 1/250 or even 1/125 sec.

Smaller subjects – especially birds, will require very fast shutter speeds. I have frozen the wing beats of dove-sized birds using 1/2000 sec. Tiny birds and insects fly so fast and erratically that even if you were able to achieve the very high shutter speeds necessary to freeze the wing beats, it is physically impossible to follow such rapid movement with a camera.

The images you may have seen of flying hummingbirds and grasshoppers, for example, will almost certainly have been taken with a infrared trip and ultra-high-speed flash. This is a complex technique requiring specialised

It always pays to be prepared. I had barely a second to grab my 300mm lens and frame the drama of this gemsbok fight – and luckily the auto-focus kicked in instantaneously! As the subjects were moving towards the camera a shutter speed of 1/500 second froze the action.

equipment – and a great deal of patience and film is bound to be wasted in getting that one great shot!

Blurred pans, on the other hand, make no attempt to freeze the subject. The technique can create a wonderful impression of speed. Typically, the background will streak as the camera follows the subject during a long exposure. If the head of the subject is fairly sharp but the rapidly moving legs or wings are blurred, this will add to the feeling of movement. Blurred pans generally work best with shutter speeds of 1/60 down to as low as 1/8 sec – again, it depends on how fast the subject is moving.

It pays to experiment. Unfortunately it is very difficult to anticipate how the final image will come out, so expect some happy surprises, along with several 'throw outs'. Blurred-pan techniques are the better option in low light, when conditions make freezing movement with a high shutter speed impossible.

A few words on equipment for shooting action. Clearly this is the area in which auto-focus lenses excel. It is possible to take action pictures with manual-focus equipment, but excellent coordination is required to pan and adjust focus at the same time; again, expect many throw outs! Even when using auto-focus, good coordination is essential to keep the focus sensing point

on the moving subject. When using lenses of 200mm and above, a fluid-action head on your tripod will make smooth, accurate panning much easier. I use a video head – the Manfrotto 136 – for all my action photography. If you have to hand-hold – such as when photographing from a moving boat – a shoulder stock support is useful.

Action opportunities are often unanticipated, fleeting and seldom repeated. Get into the habit of leaving all your cameras set on aperture priority with the widest

A fluid-action tripod head, such as this Manfrotto 136, allows smooth panning. Following action is much easier if the lens can glide effortlessly and accurately 'with' the subject.

aperture setting, therefore allowing the highest possible shutter speed. Also, always leave auto-focus set on continuous 'servo' mode. That way you will be able to grab the nearest camera and know that you can follow focus and freeze action with a high shutter speed. This has worked for me on numerous occasions, where I have picked up any camera and confidently shot fleeting action without having to waste precious seconds checking settings.

TWEAKING EXPOSURES: UNDERSTANDING HOW YOUR CAMERA 'SEES' AN IMAGE

Attaining the correct exposure has become much easier in recent years with multi-segment metering and other sophisticated systems found in modern cameras. However, even the latest and most expensive camera models do not understand how light or dark the subject should look in a photograph. For example, if you frame a great white egret, the camera does not know that the bird should appear white. It is likely to underexpose the image so that the egret is, instead, a dirty grey. Similarly, a dark subject such as a wildebeest will result in overexposure, where the animal will look grey rather than black.

It is important to understand that the camera meter reads *tone*, in other words, the degree of brightness – not colour. Very high tone elements would include bright subjects, such as fluffy white clouds and the sparkle of sunlight reflected in water. Black or dark subjects and areas of shadow (on a sunny day) are low tone.

Fortunately for wildlife photographers, most of the natural world is more or less mid-tone – such as green grass, clear blue skies and tawny-coloured lions. So if you take a picture of a lion in green grass with blue sky in the background, there is an excellent chance that the camera meter will read the image correctly. By using the exposure set by the camera, the picture should come out fine.

Situations in which you need to be careful are when there are very bright or dark areas in the composed picture, as these are likely to skew the exposure reading. If the great white egret appears large in the frame then tweaking the camera exposure by *overexposing* by a half or perhaps as much as one stop, will make the image appear white in the photograph. By the same token, dark subjects – like our wildebeest, will need an *underexposure* of between half to one stop.

Cape buffalos are dark animals so, to compensate, I underexposed this shot by one stop. Without exposure compensation the colour of these buffalos would have been recorded on the film as a washed out grey.

Very bright, high tone subjects can also skew exposures. I overexposed by a half stop to keep this spoonbill looking white.

The camera's meter generally averages the black-and-white stripes of a zebra quite accurately, so no compensation is necessary.

The angle of light also affects exposure readings. Flat-on light (with the sun directly behind you) needs the least correction. Sidelighting – particularly in harsh light – causes dense shadows. The camera will tend to average the bright and dark areas. This could result in overexposure of the brightly lit parts of the picture, so underexposing by just a half stop is often a good idea. When backlighting a subject you will want most of the picture to appear quite dark in order to accentuate the rim-lighting effect. Backlit subjects are generally best underexposed – often by as much as one full stop.

Knowing when to tweak exposures or leave well enough alone tends to be almost as much an art as a science. Experience helps a lot, as does making a few notes when you have altered an exposure.

Another important factor to take into account is the type of film that you are using.

Print (negative film) has good exposure latitude, so exposure tweaks are seldom necessary. If anything, it is easier to get a good print from a negative that is a little on the dark side, so, when in doubt, try overexposing by a stop.

Slide (transparency) film is a different story altogether. This filmstock needs very precise exposure, and even as little as a half stop off the mark will give disappointing results. The main problem with slide film is that highlight areas easily 'blow out' if overexposed. Overexposure renders the slide useless as the blow out cannot be corrected after processing. This is because there is no information on the slide that enables it to be corrected. For this reason, and, again, when in doubt, underexpose slide film by just a tad – say a half stop, or at the most two-thirds.

When shooting slides, it is also helpful to use the auto-bracket function (if your camera has one). Set the auto-bracket at a half stop either side of your selected exposure. Effectively, this means that you will be shooting three frames for every good exposure, but, if you look on the two 'wasted' exposure brackets as insurance, it is worth it.

In terms of exposure latitude, digital is a little more forgiving than slide film. Once again, overly bright or dark areas on a digital image will carry little information, so there is only so much correction that can be done later in the 'digital darkroom'.

I sat with this lioness for a couple of hours late one afternoon. Luckily she got up and began to hunt just as the light had softened to a perfect gold. I underexposed by half a stop to maintain detail in the back-lit fur and saturate the image colour.

Good, diffused light occurs during bright, overcast conditions. I photographed this young elephant calf early one cloudy but bright afternoon.

HOW TO RECOGNISE 'GOLDEN LIGHT'

Working with light is undoubtedly the key factor in making attractive and striking images.

Even the most impressive wildlife subjects can look dull and uninteresting when photographed in the flat glare of the midday sun. Although our eyes perceive detail in both the brightly lit and shadowed areas in bright, harsh light, photographic film is unable to record these extremes of contrast satisfactorily. Understanding the limitations imposed by high contrast and poor exposure latitude of film is of paramount importance.

It is, of course, widely known that the best times to photograph centre around the early morning hours and late afternoon. Wildlife photographers need to not only rise with the sparrows, but rather well before them to be in position for photography.

Both the very early morning and the late afternoon sunlight is soft and golden. This not only adds a warm glow to the photograph, but, more importantly, the lighting is soft and gentle enough to successfully light the subject from any direction.

Essentially, three options are available when choosing the lighting direction for your subject. These are, sidelighting, backlighting or flat-on, with the sun directly behind you. Each will give a distinctly different flavour and feel to the subject. Both side- and backlighting tend to produce the most visually striking images, whereas flat-on lighting is preferable when an accurate, documentary picture is required.

Sidelighting gives a pleasing depth and texture to the subject. However, it tends to work well only when the sun is very low, generally limiting this technique to the first hour after dawn and the last hour before sunset. After that, the sunlight and shadow areas of the image have greater contrast than the film can handle.

You have a little more leeway when backlighting a subject. This is successful for an hour or two of first and last light. Backlighting produces exciting rim-lit graphic images, and is a technique I like to use whenever the opportunity arises. Be careful, though, to avoid having the sun shine directly onto the lens, as this will produce flare and a misting or softening of the image.

After the magic first hour or two has passed, contrast increases dramatically, and I prefer to light a subject flat-on, with the sun directly behind me. This generally allows for another couple of hours of successful photography before conditions become too harsh for even this technique. On sunny days during the summer months and between 8am and 4pm, the light is generally too harsh for good photography, which I guess means that wildlife photographers must have the longest lunch break of any profession! During winter, the sun's angle is, of course, lower, and the good light lasts for another hour or so.

What if the sun does not shine? I often meet other photographers on my travels and am surprised that many tell me they do not even bother to photograph on dull days. I agree that the lower light levels do tend to exclude the possibility of high shutter speeds for freezing action. However, fairly bright, overcast conditions can provide a marvellous soft light for animal and bird portraits. In fact, the soft lighting is particularly suitable for photographing animals and birds in a forest environment where, under sunny conditions, the dappled light and shade makes successful photography very difficult indeed.

On cloudy days the light is strongest from mid-morning to mid-afternoon, and, because the light is diffused, this is the best time to photograph on such days.

A Kalahari meerkat poses in soft, golden light late in the afternoon. Sidelighting gives a pleasing depth and texture to the image, but requires near perfect low lighting.

When on a long photo trip, I actually welcome the odd overcast day, as it gives me a break from my regular 4.30am wake-up call, and I have an opportunity to enjoy a leisurely breakfast before starting photography at around 9am!

FILL FLASH: HOW TO FIX 'BAD LIGHT'

As I have just explained, the soft, golden sunlight is generally the best natural lighting for photography. However, to photograph only in 'good' light is pretty limiting. In mid-winter it is not so bad, as a low sun angle means that viable light lasts for an hour or two at the start

My standard set-up for using fill flash from a vehicle with the flash directed from the rear window. It is important to position the flash a short distance from the camera to avoid 'red eye'.

appearance of the image by filling in shadows and reducing contrast. The key to using flash and natural light together is to keep the flash subtle. When a photograph looks like it has obviously been taken with flash, too much light has been added. The idea is to use only the absolute minimum of flash required to correct excessive contrast and shadows. Overdo it and pictures soon start to look artificial and rather ghastly.

Most modern flash systems work 'through the lens' (TTL); in other words, the camera's internal meter measures the amount of flash light being reflected back from the subject, and switches off the flash when the required exposure has been achieved. The photographer has the option to control how much light is added by dialing in under- or overexposure on the flash.

and end of the day. But in summer the sun seems to zoom up from the horizon, and even an hour after sunrise the light is already too harsh for quality photography. Fill flash is a wonderful technique that allows you to take great pictures even when natural light has become quite harsh. With fill flash, a controlled amount of flash is added to the natural light. This greatly improves the

By the way, it is a very good idea to read the camera and flash manuals thoroughly before venturing on a field trip. The procedure for making flash exposure compensation varies with different models as well as makes. In some systems the compensation is made on the flash, while in others, flash compensation is dialed into the camera itself. Trying to figure out how all this works

The Cape fox makes an enchanting subject, but this one was in a difficult position in deep shade. Adding minus one stop of fill flash neutralised the blue tone present in shaded light.

Midday is one of the toughest times to make good pictures. I used quite heavy fill flash for the shot of this caracal, to put some detail into the dense shadows and reduce contrast.

when a cheetah is about to pounce on an impala is sure to be a frustrating experience.

Knowing how much flash to add is a bit tricky, and depends on the harshness of the sunlight at the time. When the light has become fairly bright and glaring – such as at mid-morning and afternoon, I generally dial in between minus one-and-a-half stops and minus two stops compensation into the flash. This corrects unwanted shadows and contrast without giving the picture an overly flashed, artificial appearance.

At noon, with a blazing sun directly overhead, rather more flash is required – often as much as minus one stop fill. Admittedly, the fact that quite a lot of flash has been added is then quite noticeable but, as a rule, the pictures look a great deal better than those where only natural light had been used. In any case, midday sun is an almost impossible time to take photographs. At least by using a fairly heavy amount of fill, it is possible to salvage something usable from a difficult situation.

As well as fixing contrast and shadows in harsh sunlight, fill flash can also greatly improve the appearance of a photograph in other less-than-ideal lighting situations. On an overcast day, pictures often look dull

and flat. Adding just a tiny amount of fill can lift the image and give sparkle and texture to the subject.

In overcast situations I set my flash to minus two, or even minus two-and-a-half stops. Anything more tends to look like overkill.

It is important to remember that if a flash is used on the camera hot shoe, there is a good chance that your

Fill flash helped to reduce contrast and generally 'lift' this image. Soon after taking this wide-angle shot I discovered that African penguins have powerful beaks that deliver quite a nip!

pictures will reflect the dreaded 'red eye'. The large eyes of nocturnal animals and birds are particularly susceptible to this problem.

The only way to avoid red eye is to use a dedicated connecting cable, and position the flash a metre or so to either side of the camera. This prevents the light from the flash entering the subject's eye and reflecting directly back through the camera lens.

Using off-camera flash is easy when working from a vehicle. I generally photograph from the car's front window, and point the flash out of the back window. However, in a small hide off-camera flash becomes rather cumbersome, as it is necessary to set up a separate tripod to hold the flash just outside the hide.

A limiting factor in using fill flash is the 'reach' of the flash unit. It is a good idea to run a test roll of film through your camera to check just how far away the flash is able to illuminate a subject. The flash beam intensifiers mentioned earlier under Photo Equipment are very useful, adding up to two stops more power.

While fill flash is not an easy technique to master, it greatly extends the time period for viable photography, and is therefore well worth the trouble. I find that when the light is 'bad', it interrupts my usual routine of a midday snooze on a field trip. With fill flash it is possible to take good pictures right through the day, and I have no excuse at all to take a break!

It is easy to expose for silhouettes such as this marabou stork at sunset. Simply meter off the sky close to the subject (with the camera set on manual exposure) and then reframe the image.

NIGHT PHOTOGRAPHY: DUSK TO DAWN OPPORTUNITIES

Photography during the dusk to dawn period falls into two categories. The first is the period at twilight and at dawn, when the sky colour makes it is possible to produce beautiful and evocative silhouette images using the available natural light. Then there is night photography 'proper', where a flash is the sole source of light.

Photography in the pitch black of night is very much the simpler of the two, so we will have a look at that first.

In recent years, and with the introduction of TTL ('through the lens') metering, night flash photography has become straightforward and easy. It is pretty much a case of pointing the camera at the subject and letting the on-board electronics take care of exposure. However, I think night pictures should look as if they have been taken after dark, so I dial in just a tad of underexposure to make the image appear more authentic. Usually about a half stop underexposure looks right.

As in using fill flash, the reach of the flash can be a problem, and the use of fast film and/or the flash beam intensifier mentioned previously can increase range.

These Kalahari lions presented a tricky exposure. I metered off the sky and underexposed a half stop. Fill flash, directed at the lions, was added at minus one stop to maintain the dawn atmosphere.

Nocturnal creatures are especially prone to the 'red-eye' effect if you use a flash on the camera hot shoe. For this Cape eagle owl portrait I used a big flash held off camera on a bracket. The set-up is unwieldy, but gives pleasing results.

Focusing at night is tricky, and for this reason it is helpful to have a second person operate a spotlight. I also tape a powerful torch onto the camera bracket holding the flash, so there is some illumination wherever the camera is pointed. I always use my fastest lens for night work – a 300mm f2.8 – as the bright image makes focusing easier. With both the spotlight and the torch trained on the subject, there is usually sufficient light to allow the camera's auto-focus to operate.

The half-light periods at dusk and dawn offer great opportunities for exciting bird silhouettes, not only of nocturnal species such as owls, but also of roosting diurnal birds.

Animal silhouettes are also possible if you can frame the subject against the skyline. Exposures can be difficult as the camera meter may be fooled into overexposing if a lot of the dark subject appears in frame. The result is a washed-out sky and a grey rather than black silhouette.

The best way to guarantee correct exposure is to take a reading from the sky close to the subject, and then reframe the picture. Most cameras have an exposure lock facility that ensures that the exposure will not change when the picture is reframed.

I prefer to simply set the camera to manual exposure, set the sky exposure and then frame the subject. Just to be on the safe side, I also bracket exposures and take a few shots at a half stop below the meter reading as well. This saturates the sky colour and also makes the silhouette image appear in graphic detail. Light levels are, of course, very low at this time of day, resulting in long exposures.

To produce crisp, sharp images it is essential to avoid any camera shake or unsteadiness. By using a heavy tripod and a cable release I have managed to get away with exposures as slow as a half second, even when using a 600mm telephoto lens. Even the tiny vibration caused by the internal mirror in the camera flipping up just prior to the shutter firing can spoil a picture. In telephoto photography, mirror flip-up vibration is most noticeable at speeds between 1/30 and one-half second. When using telelenses of 300mm or longer at these shutter speeds it is a good idea to use the mirror lock-up facility – if your camera has one. This completely solves the vibration problem as it allows the mirror to be manually locked up well before you fire the shutter.

The fill flash techniques described earlier can also be used to great effect at twilight and at dawn.

I set my camera exposure to manual and take a sky reading – exactly as I would to make a silhouette. I then dial in around one-stop underexposure into the flash. The idea here is to capture the wonderful twilight/dawn atmosphere, rather than to artificially create a daylight effect, so that underexposure in the flash looks more convincing. Although this technique may sound a bit complicated and confusing, it is well worth getting the hang of it. It is one of my favourites and is a great way to produce striking and unusual images.

In the past, only the upmarket, expensive private game lodges offered night drives, which was very restricting for a person on a limited budget wishing to do some night photography. Fortunately, many of South Africa's national parks now offer escorted night drives, so that everyone has an opportunity to try this interesting branch of wildlife photography.

WIDE-ANGLE PHOTOGRAPHY:
HOW TO LINK A SUBJECT
WITH ITS ENVIRONMENT

There is a a trick to getting the most out of a wide-angle lens. A lot of folk imagine that, as a wide-angle lens has a wide view, it will take great pictures of landscapes – right?

The answer is at best, 'not necessarily'.

Wide angles may enable you to capture a wide vista, but they also greatly alter and stretch perspective. A mountain range may look impressive to the eye, but take a shot with a 24mm lens and the scene will be far less dramatic; for a start, the mountains will appear smaller

I wanted to use the stream as a foreground subject in this 17mm wide-angle Drakensberg landscape. I set up my tripod in the stream, and had wet hiking boots for the rest of the day!

I used a 20mm lens to link these Namib fog-drinking beetles with their desert environment. I had to stop down to f22 to maintain sharpness throughout the image.

and more distant. With a wide angle, what you see with your eye is not at all what will result in a picture.

The trick with using a wide angle is to *always include a subject of interest in the foreground*. This will provide a feeling of depth and perspective to the image. My favourite use of wide angles is to show a subject in its environment. This offers a unique kind of imagery that would be impossible with any other type of lens.

Useful foreground subjects include flowers or other interesting plants, and even attractive rocks.

Less-mobile, small fauna can also work well. Suitable wide-angle fauna subjects are those that do not run away, or have a tendency to bite the photographer! Tortoises are good, along with chameleons, frogs and any other docile reptiles.

To link a subject with its background you will generally need to get low and very close, because a wide angle will tend to make everything look smaller and further away – including the foreground subject. It pays to experiment with different angles and distances, which is why fauna subjects need to be accommodating!

To avoid getting your shadow in the picture it is often necessary to use cross-light when working with wide angles. I added soft fill from a gold reflector on the tsamma melon in the foreground.

Most successful wide-angle shots require great depth of field so go for small apertures of f16 or f22. This should enable you to get both the foreground subject and a distant vista in sharp focus. Small apertures mean slow shutter speeds, so be sure to use a tripod when you take a picture. However, hand-hold for maximum mobility when experimenting with framing the image. Only set up the tripod when you are satisfied that you have found the best camera position.

On occasion, large mammal species can also make good wide-angle subjects. For obvious reasons it is not wise to try this on foot; photographing from a vehicle is safer. Your subjects should also be well habituated, and tolerant of vehicles and close human presence.

When positioning the camera, be careful to avoid including your own shadow in the picture, a mistake easily made when working with super-wide lenses. This means shooting with cross-light much of the time, so harsh contrast can be a problem.

A fill flash, described earlier, and reflector (discussed later under Close-up Photography) can both help. Of course, it is only possible to fill the foreground shadows, but this can improve the image enormously. Given a choice of the two fill methods, I generally prefer a reflector, as you can see the effect on the image in the viewfinder. Flash always involves a certain amount of guesswork, as you will only know exactly how the fill looks after the film is processed.

CLOSE-UP PHOTOGRAPHY: A WEALTH OF OPPORTUNITY IN YOUR BACK GARDEN

Close-up nature photography opens up a fascinating range of opportunities, and the nice thing about it is that there are plenty of interesting subjects to be found in your own back garden. And, you don't have to wait for a visit to the game reserve to indulge in this wonderful pastime. Typical gardens subjects include flowers and other botanical specimens, butterflies, bugs and small reptiles.

Producing quality close-up images can be fairly challenging, and requires a meticulous approach to camera work and lighting. We will examine close-up camera techniques in a moment, but first let's take a look at the gear you will need.

A standard 50mm lens can make excellent close-up images. All you will need to add is a set of extension tubes to make the lens focus more closely.

An extension tube contains no optics, and is, fortunately, a fairly inexpensive accessory. For a 50mm lens the most useful tube lengths are 15mm and 25mm. Another option is to use a 70–200mm zoom that has a 'macro' facility. This allows the zoom to focus a bit closer than normal, although there does tend to be some loss

I photographed this swallowtail butterfly in my back garden. A 70–200mm telephoto zoom helped blur a distracting garden background, and gave the image a 'natural' appearance.

The 'worm's-eye view' often works with small subjects. This Namaqua chameleon was photographed with a 100mm macro supported by a beanbag about 3cm above ground level.

of image quality. These lenses contain very complex optics, and it is difficult for the manufacturers to design a zoom that works optimally at both close-up and normal ranges.

If you don't mind spending a fair amount of cash, then a true macro lens will make the job much easier. Macro lenses focus very close without having to add an extension tube. These specialist lenses are built to perform best at close range, so image quality is outstanding.

You can use either natural light or a flash for close-ups. Natural light is generally easier as it is possible see in the viewfinder exactly how the image will appear.

Depth of field is very limited, so small apertures – f11, f16 or even f22 – are necessary to get the entire subject in sharp focus. If your camera has a stop-down button this will be handy to check the depth of field before you take a picture. As always, small apertures mean slow shutter speeds, so a tripod and cable release are essential – exactly the same as for telephoto photography.

If the light is too harsh, or even a little flat, the image can be improved greatly by using a reflector. A reflector held close to the subject will fill hard shadows on a bright day, and can also add a little sparkle in overcast conditions. You can buy collapsible reflectors from a camera store, but an A4-size gold or silver card is equally effective, and a great deal cheaper.

Natural light close-ups generally look best when shot at an angle that allows a distant, out-of-focus background. The subject then stands out clearly with minimum background clutter.

One problem with natural light is that the subject must be perfectly still to avoid blurring. Bugs that crawl or fly away are a hassle. Even flower photography is almost impossible on a windy day. At times I have waited half an hour for a lull in the wind before being able to take a shot.

The very brief duration of flash completely solves the problem of subject movement and will allow you to hand-hold the camera, so there is no need to bother with a tripod. This mobility helps when trying to cope with a lively bug or reptile. If you have TTL ('through the lens') metering, flash exposures are straightforward. Use a small

It pays to look down for macro subjects. Sea shells in soft, overcast light always offer promising studies in composition.

Harsh sunlight on close-up subjects is easily fixed with a gold reflector. I used a 100mm macro on these impala lilies at midday.

A polarising filter greatly increases saturation in a blue sky, giving more impact to the fluffy white clouds at De Hoop Nature Reserve.
A polariser also reduces reflection and glare from water. Without the filter this late morning seascape would have appeared flat and dull.

aperture for depth of field, and the camera's electronics will take care of the exposure.

Non-TTL flash systems – which tend to be the older or cheaper models – require manual exposures. The best way to deal with this is to set the flash manually to full power, use a small camera aperture, and run a series of close-up test shots at a fixed distance with varying apertures. Once you have found the precise distance for correct exposure at a given aperture, it will always be possible to repeat these results.

USING FILTERS TO ENHANCE NATURAL COLOUR

Filters should be used much like the fill flash techniques discussed earlier. In both cases, 'less is more'. In other words, if you show a picture to some friends and they say, 'Oh, we see that you have used a filter!' then you have probably overdone it.

My feeling is that 'special effect' filters such as starbursts or strongly coloured graduated filters have no place in nature photography. The results tend to look both gimmicky and clichéd.

I use only two types of filter, and then as sparingly as possible, the idea being to bring the photographic image

as close as possible to how I perceived the scene with my eye, rather than attempting to add colours or effects that were never there in the first place.

First on the list is the polarising filter. It is well known that these filters saturate blue skies. The effect is wonderful at low altitudes and especially in a hazy or dusty atmosphere. A pale, weak-coloured sky can be saturated to a deep but convincing blue.

A polarising filter works best at about 90° to the sun. You will need to rotate the filter in its holder until maximum polarisation is achieved.

Most photographers tend to use a polarising filter for wide-angle landscapes. If you are shooting with a 70–200mm zoom and include sky in the image, it is also worth experimenting with this filter. The narrower angle of view of a short telephoto zoom means that the sky included is close to the horizon, and generally of the palest blue. Polarising can really help enhance the sky in these shots. Better yet, partly cloudy days with odd patches of blue sky can look fantastic when polarised with any focal length lens. Be sure to give this a try.

Polarising filters have a couple of other useful applications. One is to reduce reflections in water. Sometimes this is desirable and on other occasions not,

I used a two-stop graduated neutral density filter to darken only the top half of this bush fire image. This enhanced the smoky sky, and brought the foreground glowing embers within film latitude.

so check out the effect in the viewfinder first. Also, and this is a less widely known but nonetheless handy technique, try polarising foliage and forest scenes. Even on cloudy days, polarising reduces leaf shine, and so saturates and enhances the natural greens.

While on the subject of polarising filters, I should mention a couple of points to watch out for. Firstly, when polarising an already deep blue sky, be careful that you don't overdo it. In particular, if you are using a highly saturated film, adding polarisation can go right over the top, and you could end up with a horrible, unnatural ultramarine/black sky! This is most noticeable at high altitudes. For example, when I shoot clear-weather scenics in the Drakensberg range, I no longer use a polarising filter; the effect is too much and looks artificial.

Also, be careful when using this filter on a super-wide lens. Because polarisation is greatest at 90° to the sun the sky may appear deep blue on one side of the picture and much paler on the other. The effect looks decidedly odd, so try to avoid it.

A graduated neutral density filter is also a good investment. I use a 'grad' filter infrequently, but in certain

conditions it can really save the day or, at least, the shot. This filter is designed to overcome high contrast situations that are beyond the latitude of film.

A good example is when photographing a landscape on a cloudy day. If you expose to maintain detail in the landscape, then the sky is likely to bleach out to a boring, unattractive white. Aligning the dark part of a grad filter over the sky will bring out texture in the sky without altering the rest of the scene. Being of neutral density, these filters do not shift the colour, so everything stays nice and natural-looking.

A last word on filters. Some photographers leave a UV filter permanently fitted to their lens. The UV makes almost no discernible difference to the picture and primarily acts to protect the lens from scratches.

I'm not the most careful of folk but in 20 years of photography I have yet to put a scratch on a lens element. I have put plenty of scratches – and several dents – on lens casings, but have yet to damage the optics.

I have never, therefore, bothered with a UV filter but, if you prefer to fit one for 'insurance' and peace of mind, then go for it.

As well as saturating blue skies, a polariser can also help boost the natural greens in foliage by cutting through leaf shine. I used a 17mm lens and polariser for this Tsitsikamma forest scene.

*Although I could have framed this Kalahari lion a lot tighter by using a 600mm lens, I chose instead to use my 300mm and a 1.4×
converter (420mm). Aside from showing something of the lion's habitat, the trees on the left provide a pleasing balance to the picture.*

COMPOSITION: THE ART OF 'MAKING' PICTURES RATHER THAN JUST 'TAKING' THEM

The art of making a picture lies, essentially, in its
composition. This subject has been studied intensively in
the wider field of the visual arts and in photography. There
have been many attempts to define 'rules' or 'formulas' in
composing a pleasing picture. A well known example is
the 'Rule of Thirds', whereby the picture rectangle is
divided by horizontal and vertical lines splitting the area
into thirds. Where the lines intersect is deemed to be an
optimal position for the subject of the picture. Granted,
being a little off centre (top left, top right, bottom left or
bottom right) can lead to a pleasing composition.

Using the Rule of Thirds excessively can also look a bit
contrived. I believe there need only be one rule of
composition and that is simply to *experiment*. All the
other so-called rules are really just made to be broken.

When you come across a photo subject – and it could
be anything from a tiny mushroom to a magnificent
leopard – it is a good idea to quickly fire off a couple of
frames. This overcomes the mental obstacle of needing to
get something 'in the bag'. After that you can relax, have
fun and, as I said before, experiment.

Ask yourself 'What if...?'

*Chacma baboons photographed near Skukuza. I thought the
mother and baby interaction provided a most interesting
opportunity, and made some tight shots with a 600mm.*

Diagonal lines tend to create a visual dynamic in a picture, although I have to admit that capturing this bateleur's take-off at such an angle was sheer luck! A 1/750 sec shutter speed on my 600mm f4 lens froze the action.

Examples would be, 'What if I try a lower or higher camera angle?' Or, 'What if I put a teleconverter onto my longest lens and try for a really tight detail shot, or use a wide lens to show something of the habitat of the subject?'

The possibilities and combinations are infinite. Try a flash or reflector. Experiment with side- or backlighting. Use a smaller aperture for plenty of depth of field – or the other way around. Also, try framing the subject off-centre. Usually it looks best to have some empty space for an animal to look at, walk towards or run into. But not always … as I said rules are made to be broken!

Another point to remember when composing an image, is that diagonal lines in the picture generally look more dynamic than horizontals or verticals. As an example, if you were to photograph a chameleon crawling along a horizontal branch, the picture would have a static feel. However, frame the branch as a diagonal and it would give a greater impression of movement. The picture would appear more dynamic and would give the impression that the chameleon is going somewhere. You can achieve this by bending the branch down a bit (but you might just upset the chameleon in the process!), or simply angle the camera. The result will appear the same. Just be careful to avoid including a clear horizon as a background as this will look decidedly odd if 'tilted'.

You only need to shoot a frame or two of each of these 'experiments'. Film is not cheap these days, but compared to the expense of having the opportunity to take the picture in the first place (if you include fuel, reserve entry fees and accommodation), the cost is not excessive. Take a good look at the results when you get home, decide which shots you like and then try to figure out why they work.

Don't get too bogged down with technical perfection, after all, with today's 'auto-everything' cameras it is not all that difficult to take technically competent pictures. The important thing is that the image says something about how you felt about the subject, and these images tend to be the ones you 'make' through experimenting.

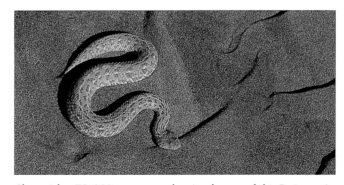

Shot with a 70–200mm zoom, the visual story of this Peringuey's adder and its sand patterns made a better composition at the shorter end of the zoom range – around 100mm.

PRIME PHOTOGRAPHIC
RESERVES IN SOUTH AFRICA

Augrabies Falls National Park is one of the best locations in South Africa in which to photograph the enchanting Klipspringer.

Cape sugarbirds are present in many reserves in the western Cape, including Kirstenbosch Gardens and Helderberg Nature Reserve.

There are numerous excellent travel guidebooks that describe South Africa's game and nature reserves, but few, if any of them cover what every keen photographer needs to know.

Which are the reserves that offer the best wildlife photographic opportunities? What times of the year are best for photography, and what species are you likely to photograph most successfully in each reserve?

The list of locations offered below makes no attempt at being comprehensive, but rather highlights the areas in South Africa that I visit regularly and have found to be consistently productive.

In addition to our national parks, South Africa is dotted with numerous smaller provincial nature reserves. These are also certainly worth visiting, as even the tiny nature reserves have photographic possibilities if you take the time to look carefully.

ADDO ELEPHANT NATIONAL PARK

An excellent location for elephant photography throughout the year. It is generally easy to find the big breeding herds, but especially easy in hot weather as the elephants make regular visits to the water holes. Great for action photography!

It is usually possible to get good images of red hartebeest and ostrich here as well. Addo also has a population of meerkats, but you will need a little luck to get within viable camera range. Likewise, buffalos and black rhinos, although present, are seldom seen close to the tourist roads.

AUGRABIES FALLS NATIONAL PARK

Of course everyone who visits Augrabies photographs the magnificent falls. Generally, maximum flows take place in the first four months of the year. Game is mostly sparse, but klipspringers are common and probably easier to photograph here than anywhere else in South Africa. There is some interesting flora, including quiver trees. Augrabies is worth a visit at any time of the year, but summers are very hot!

CAPE PENINSULA NATIONAL PARK

While the entire Peninsula National Park is great for coastal scenics and fynbos flora, there are rather limited opportunities for game and bird photography. Wind is a real problem; try not to visit when the Cape south-easter is howling!

Addo is productive right through the year. However, hot summer days may encourage the big breeding herds to visit water holes – with lots of opportunities for action shots.

The Kgalagadi's camps can be a good place to spot owls. These spotted eagle owl chicks were photographed at Twee Rivieren.

A herd of blue wildebeest follows the dry Nossob riverbed near Twee Rivieren camp in the Kgalagadi.

The Kgalagadi is prime predator habitat, but be prepared to put in a lot of driving for good photo opportunities.

Boulders Beach, is a good photographic location in Cape Town, if you are looking for great shots of the endangered African penguin.

If you want to photograph the beautiful, long-tailed Cape sugarbirds feeding on proteas, then **Kirstenbosch Botanical Gardens** on Table Mountain, and **Helderberg Nature Reserve** in Somerset West are a good bet in spring and early summer.

DRAKENSBERG RESERVES

The best way to explore and photograph this extensive area is on foot. In fact, it is often necessary to embark on a long hike to get to the best scenic spots. Avoid late-winter visits, when veld-burning produces haze, making good scenic photography impossible. At any other time of the year – and especially just after rain – the Drakensberg air positively sparkles.

If time is limited and you don't feel like lugging a heavy camera bag over miles of trails, then the **Royal Natal National Park** is the most accessible venue. Classic shots of the Amphitheatre can be taken from the Tugela River valley, just a few minutes' walk from the road.

Other short trails lead to waterfalls, tree ferns and Berg vistas – all great for photography.

Giant's Castle is outstanding for bird photography. The reserve's excellent Vulture Hide is renowned for its black eagle, jackal buzzard and lanner falcon sightings, as well as visits by the stunning bearded vulture. The hide is very popular, so bookings need to be made well in advance.

The rest camp at Giant's Castle has resident sunbirds and Guerney's sugarbird; all are fairly habituated and approachable for photography. Eland are often seen close to the camp in the winter months.

In the southern Free State, **Golden Gate Highlands National Park** offers easy access for scenic shots, as well as spring and summer flower photography.

KGALAGADI TRANSFRONTIER PARK

This area, part of which was formerly known as the Kalahari Gemsbok National Park, is a great favourite among photographers, although first-time visitors should be warned that it is an arid area with naturally low game densities. However, the brooding storm skies and dazzling sunsets, along with crisp desert light, make the Kgalagadi an outstanding photographic location. As a rule, you will need to put in a lot of time and driving for good sightings. Lion and cheetah are regularly encountered and, with a little luck, you might even see a leopard.

The best time to photograph predators tends to be in the hottest months – November to March. General game herds – gemsbok, springbok and wildebeest – usually peak in March to May, following good rains. Black-backed jackal, Cape and bat-eared foxes, and the Kalahari's wonderful meerkats can also be photographed from the road; again, putting in time is the key.

The three rest camps – Twee Rivieren, Mata Mata and Nossob – are all worth a visit. I rate Nossob and Mata Mata as equally productive for photography, with Twee Rivieren coming in a close third.

Take a break from driving and photograph the tame ground squirrel, and the yellow mongooses and small bird species that frequent the rest camps. Also, Dalkeith (Mata Mata) and Cubique (Nossob) water holes are packed with flocks of sandgrouse in the mornings.

KRUGER NATIONAL PARK

Many keen photographers stay away from Kruger in favour of the less popular reserves. This is largely because serious photography in Kruger can be frustrating due to the very high visitor numbers. In fact, lion 'traffic jams' are a common sight, with as many as 40 cars jostling for a view of this most popular of beasts.

That is not to say that successful photo opportunities do not exist in Kruger; it simply requires a different mind set. Yes, you are going to find it impossible to get a clear view of a subject at times, and you may even get crowded out of a sighting on occasion. On the more positive side, however, game in Kruger is so incredibly relaxed and habituated to vehicles that exceptionally intimate, close-up wildlife pictures can be taken. Kruger has a wonderful diversity of animals and birds so there is always something interesting to photograph – you just have to learn to work around the crowds! To avoid the crush, stay away at peak holiday times, especially the June/July school holidays.

I have done some of my best photography from the smaller bush camps at Kruger. These are situated some distance from the main camps, so the surrounding roads are very quiet in the early and later hours of the day. Excellent bush camps for photography include Mbyamiti, Talamati and Bateleur. All three camps are good for the 'big five', as well as other predators and general game.

Of the large camps, Lower Sabie, Crocodile Bridge, Skukuza, Satara and Shingwedzi are all very productive. Satara is generally regarded as the first choice for cats, although I have often done just as well at Lower Sabie and Crocodile Bridge. The Kanniedood Dam, situated

A chilly sunrise over Kruger in August. Game concentrations and photography are generally best in the winter months.

The Kruger Park offers excellent opportunities to photograph young spotted hyena at roadside dens.

Sunset Dam near Lower Sabie is a great place for water birds. Kingfishers, jacanas and herons are often within camera range, along with the marabou stork shown here.

right next to Shingwedzi camp, is one of the most prolific elephant photography hot-spots in the Park.

Kruger is worth visiting throughout the year, although both predators and plains game are most concentrated in the dry season – June to October. While Kruger has an already abundant birdlife, summer sees the arrival of many migratory species, including the woodland kingfisher.

Explore the camp grounds and picnic sites for habituated birds. Various hornbill species, glossy starlings and colourful barbets are often so tame that they can

easily be photographed with a 200mm lens. Keep a lookout for dwarf and banded mongooses, both of which tend to be habituated and easily approachable. Reptiles also offer rewarding opportunities, and agama lizards are common in the wooded areas at most camps.

MOUNTAIN ZEBRA NATIONAL PARK

Famed for the preservation of the highly endangered Cape mountain zebra, this small park is well worth a visit. In addition to the mountain zebra, expect to photograph red hartebeest and a variety of birdlife. I've had some great shots of malachite sunbirds right in the rest camp. Most of the game is to be found on the high plateau above the camp – an area that is productive all year round. In mid-winter it sometimes snows; shots of a mountain zebra in the snow would be quite something!

PILANESBURG

One of the great conservation success stories of South Africa, Pilanesberg now holds a good game density. The reserve offers a rare opportunity to photograph both black and white rhino. 'Big five' sightings are frequent, and general game and bird photography is good.

The reserve is very busy over weekends and during school holidays. Visit mid-week and off-season, and you should have peace and quiet and plenty of photo subjects that are habituated to vehicles. Pilanesberg is productive all year round. Summers are hot, but unlike the Lowveld, not too oppressive. Also, being malaria-free means that Pilanesberg is a good, safe bet during the warmer months.

RICHTERSVELD AND NAMAQUALAND

I reckon that the Richtersveld is about as isolated a spot as it is possible to find in South Africa. Stunning mountain views – the Richtersveld is the only mountainous desert in

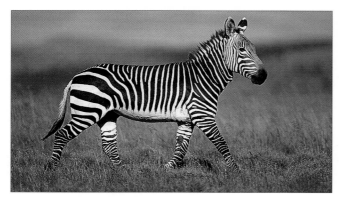

Mountain Zebra Park is a productive location for red hartebeest, as well as the rare zebra species after which the Park is named.

Winter-flowering aloes attract glossy starlings (shown here), sunbirds, bulbuls, and orioles to Kruger's rest camps.

The Richtersveld is a wonderfully remote area to explore. This is a dawn scene from Potjiespram camp site.

On only a few occasions have I had the elusive finfoot within telephoto range at Hluhluwe and the Kruger Park.

South Africa – plus good scenics along the Orange River make this a prime photo location. Fascinating succulent plant species include the halfmens and quiver tree.

Although taking photographs in the Richtersveld is not restricted to any specific time of year, remember that summer temperatures often exceed 40°C. This is not the place to go if you want to photograph animals, as game is sparse and skittish. Small bird species, such as chats, robins and francolins, are, however, very confiding in the camping areas. The Richtersveld requires a reliable four-wheel drive and good advance planning.

Kamieskroon is a good base from which to explore the world-famous spring flowers of Namaqualand. The area is far more accessible, and you can easily do the trip in an ordinary car. Flowers bloom only for a short period every year, anytime from mid-August to early October, depending on rainfall.

TSITSIKAMMA

Both the forest and coastline at Tsitsikamma are primarily scenic photographic destinations. Animals, apart from the odd bushbuck, are scarce, and forest birds – such as the colourful Knysna lourie – are usually exceedingly difficult to photograph.

On a dull day it pays to head for the forest to try your hand at scenic images. Soft, overcast light eliminates shadows and makes for great forest interiors – shots that are impossible in dappled light on a sunny day. Sparkling forest streams, ancient yellowwoods and bright green ferns make good wide-angle images. Take along your macro gear for close-ups of plants, frogs and other small reptiles that you are sure to encounter on the forest trails.

When the sun shines, head for the Tsitsikamma coast for scenics. Try to arrive early or stay late to make the most of the light.

ZULULAND RESERVES

Of all the Zululand Reserves, **Mkuze** is the prime photo location. During the dry June to October period, excellent game hides allow easy water-hole photography. Expect a procession of animals including white rhinos, nyalas, zebras, wildebeest and baboons. Nsumo Pan, also at Mkuze, sometimes offers good opportunities to photograph pelicans and hippos, although you may need a long lens.

Hluhluwe-Umfolozi Park is probably the number one location in South Africa for white rhino photography. There are also lots of elephants here, as well as an assortment of general game. In the summer months, when long grass makes viewing difficult, try the Seme area in southern Hluhluwe. The close-cropped grass at Seme offers clear views for excellent white rhino photography, along with plenty of general game.

Game numbers have improved greatly in recent years at **Ithala**, and both black and white rhinos are seen here regularly. Although lions are absent, other general game is prolific. You can usually spot plenty at Ithala all year round, but from a photographic point of view avoid February to April, when the grass is longest.

Tsitsikamma is a great place for dramatic seascapes. I used a 70–200mm zoom lens for this late afternoon shot.

10 GAME-VIEWING TIPS THAT WILL HELP YOU TAKE BETTER WILDLIFE PHOTOGRAPHS

Dust, late afternoon light, and wildebeest make an atmospheric scene in the Kgalagadi. The image was taken on a hot day in March when animal activity peaked early in the mornings and again late in the day.

GAME HOT SPOTS

When you arrive at a game reserve, make a point of talking to reserve staff as well as other visitors regarding the latest whereabouts of game. During the dry season it is not unusual to find up to 80 per cent of the big game species in less than 20 per cent of the reserve. Even during the summer months, when water is abundant, certain areas may offer particularly favourable grazing, and so attract big herds. Finding the game 'hot spots' is essential to productive photography.

WEATHER CONDITIONS

Weather, and particularly temperature, will affect game activity. Generally, in very hot, sunny weather the best times for photography will be in the early and late part of the day. Fortunately, this coincides with the main hours of animal activity, particularly the big cats. At mid-morning, head for a water hole; you might find a herd of thirsty elephants doing the same. Rhino, buffalo and warthog are all fond of mud-wallowing, and are also likely to be found at a water hole trying to cool off at this time of day.

GAME-DRIVES

In cool, overcast weather, animal activity may continue throughout the day. Start your game drive a little later in the morning, and continue through the midday period. Overcast light will be best for photography between 9am and 3pm.

THE ROAD

When game-viewing just for pleasure, it pays to drive slowly. When you are specifically on the lookout for animals to photograph, you should drive *extra slow*, so that you don't spook potential subjects that are close to the road.

THE APPROACH

Watch the animal carefully as you approach. If you think it shows any signs of unease, stop the vehicle, but leave the engine running. Allow the animal time to become used to the presence of your vehicle at a distance before you attempt to move closer. If you take your time, and approach with a series of slow movements, you will often be able to get within easy camera reach of even quite skittish game. Don't switch off the engine until you are in a good position to take a picture.

PROXIMITY

Don't push your luck! If the animal is clearly unhappy with your close proximity then back off. Stressed animals make bad photo subjects, and it always shows in the picture. Not only that, but stressing is bad for the animal, and it could be bad for you too because a cornered or threatened subject may charge your vehicle! Also, please don't be tempted to illegally drive off-road for a closer view. This is not allowed in most southern African reserves. You could be in for a hefty fine if caught, and the noise of off-road driving will very likely scare off the animal anyway.

ANTICIPATION

Anticipate action so that you can be ready for the shot. Most animals display 'intention movements'. For example, a lioness about to strike will crouch, ready to spring on her prey. A heron will peer intently into the water and possibly move its head a little from side to side before spearing a tilapia. When observing a subject, you need to be at the ready, with your finger on the shutter button and the motor drive set on high speed.

A cheetah chasing and killing its prey is a very difficult action shot – and one that I have yet to master! The best advice I can offer is to look at the cheetah, then at the prey, and try to anticipate in which direction the chase will go. Cheetahs frequently chase their prey for upwards of 500 metres, so you will need an enormous amount of luck, as well as excellent camera work to get this shot!

REST CAMPS

Many of the rest camps and picnic spots at South Africa's reserves draw a wide variety of birdlife. 'Resident' species – particularly sunbirds, barbets, weavers, starlings and hornbills, will be accustomed to the presence of humans, making them easy to approach and photograph.

Good macro subjects are also plentiful in rest camp areas, so be on the lookout for interesting insects, reptiles and flora.

COMMON GAME SPECIES

We all encounter slow days (or even weeks!) when searching for photo subjects. Rather than endure the tedium of endlessly searching for an elusive leopard or absent lions, take a break and photograph the more common game species. Impala, baboons and monkeys are usually easy to find, and offer wonderful behavioural photography opportunities.

NIGHT PHOTOGRAPHY

You don't need to put away your cameras when the sun goes down. As mentioned previously, a number of South Africa's reserves offer night drives, and, aside from this opportunity for night photography, nocturnal animals often patrol rest camp perimeter fences. Take a stroll around the inside of the perimeter fence with a torch an hour or so after dark, when you may get good civet and hyena pictures – even if you have to shoot through the holes in the fence.

A powerful flash is essential when photographing distant subjects at night; alternatively, use a very fast film to get more reach with a smaller flash.

The bizarre halfmens is an interesting subject for photographers visiting the Richtersveld. The most accessible specimens are to be found a few kilometres from Potjiespram camp site.

INDEX